The Crazy People From Cleveland

By Carl E. Miller

Story #1: Out of the Ordinary, in Ohio

Story #2: Demon Rats: A Shocking Journey into the Liberal Pits of America

Out of the Ordinary, in Ohio

Chapter 1: (Jack of all trades)

Chapter 2: (In broad daylight)

Chapter 3: (Good grief)

Chapter 4: (Last of a dying breed)

Introduction:

When writing a story on strange people you soon come to understand the old saying, "No sense makes sense". While observing the person of interest you begin to wonder were they ever normal at some point of their life, then you find yourself attempting to tackle the meaning of normal.

Is anyone ever really normal? I wondered this as I sat in the passenger seat of an old, yellow Chevy truck as we sped through the dark dirty streets of Cleveland at one in the morning. I started to contemplate what I was still doing here, then I glanced over at Jack who was mumbling the lyrics to David Allan Coe's hit song If That Ain't Country.

 Jack was driving the old yellow truck fiercely, gripping the wheel tightly without ever taking his eyes off the road. He drove with such passion that I still have yet to see it matched. He was a tall guy that stood about six foot three and was extremely hyper at all times. He was a real thrill seeker with never a dull moment and despite knowing him for only four months, he felt like family.

Chapter 1: Jack of all trades

"Slow down man, before you draw heat!" I shouted after catching a glimpse of the speedometer. Jack was driving sixty miles per hour down Lorain avenue, which had a limit of twenty five. He said nothing, seeming to not be listening before finally exclaiming very calmly "Hell yes" but maintained the same speed.

Without warning Jack locked his brakes and turned sharply, plowing through the bushes in front of a fast food chain before inching his way to the drive-thru speaker as a geeky voice poured out, "How can I help you?"

Jack ordered a few hamburgers then he began nudging my arm and laughing uncontrollably, demanding into the speaker that they, "make our food to go!".

"What?" replied the confused server.

After much hesitation I joined the conversation "Never mind him, he's lacking sleep" I pause briefly "just get the order ready we're in a real hurry".

"I never knew your alter ego was Captain fucking buzzkill" Jack exclaimed while still laughing. When we reached the window Jack, still didn't hit his thrill threshold, handed the server a twenty dollar bill and declared "be careful it's still wet", hinting that it was just printed illegally.

The server was now becoming angry but Jack wasn't finished "man them bushes up front look like shit, I can get them looking good again for a fair price".

Scenes like this occurred often while riding with Jack, he meant no harm but acting erratic and unpredictable was a strong trait that he possessed. The snow was falling heavy now and it was cold in his little yellow truck that had no heat, and a spider web cracked windshield. Hell I don't even think the truck had legitimate plates, I know his driver license was no longer valid, too many speeding tickets saw that.

I recall the first day I met Jack, it was much warmer then, sitting in the bleachers of Nautica pavilion in the flats, attending an Alice Cooper concert. Oddy enough at this time Jack was likely the most well-behaved person in the crowd of crazed freaks, this is why I found it rather odd when he approached me with a very attractive woman who just stuck her tiny hand out and said "Jack would really like it if you would take this", to which I obliged.

Before I knew it I was under the influence of LSD, talking it up with two complete strangers who introduced themselves as Jack and Sabrina. After telling them everything about myself and what I was doing in Cleveland I began to feel Sabrina tugging at my arm, insisting I meet Gerald.

This was the moment I realized they had a third member in their party, as Sabrina led me towards a small man. The man who I assumed to be Gerald was standing in the dark corner alone, with a crazy look in his eyes. He was wearing old, ragged clothes that were multiple sizes too small and had a long beard that was twisted together like some sort of twenty-first century wizard.

Chapter 2: In broad daylight

Gerald appeared to be in his early fifties and was obviously very paranoid, so I felt thankful when Sabrina eased into the introduction. She simply repeated what I told her and Jack moments earlier, just more simplified, leaving out only minor details.

"This is Tucker!" Sabrina proclaimed excitedly while looking at Gerald before continuing, "he came all the way from Nashville for some magazine called Volunteer's Variety, they're paying him to attend live concerts and take some pictures at the Rock Hall, isn't that nice?" She asked as he nodded.

I extended my arm, attempting to shake Gerald's hand but ignored the gesture and instead began to rant incredibly like a prime Alex Jones. "Sometimes I ride my bicycle down the worst dead-end streets in Cleveland, just for the experience. Do you ever do stuff like that?" he asked.

"No" I replied but he wasn't done rambling yet.

"Ya know I used to own a small mansion on the east side until this scumbag had it foreclosed" he paused briefly, "the man was found dead I'm his basement a month later, but I don't believe in casting spells" he said this while grinning maniacally.

"Okay" I mumbled as I began to feel confused and a bit uncomfortable. The LSD was kicking into overdrive and I noticed Sabrina abandoned us and returned to Jack, leaving me with my burden.

Gerald wasn't finished with where he was in his story, but was courteous enough to pause while Alice Cooper played a very heavy version of his classic hit I'm Eighteen that sent the crowd into a frenzy, immediately after the song finished Gerald impatiently resumed.

"So now I moved to the west side which I assumed would be much quieter, but proved to be wrong".

"Why did it prove to be wrong?" I asked, not really caring but not wanting to be rude.

"Some guy started parking his R.V in the street directly in front of my house, he had a dog that barked all hours of the day. Eventually I grew so tired of it that I called the cops and told them he was out there fucking his dog in broad daylight, nearly an hour later I could hear shouting outside".

"Who said I was fucking my dog? God damn it!, the man in the R.V yelled at two police officers as he looked around in anger. Moments later he burned his tires, driving away pointing at every house and screaming crazily".

Gerald was laughing so hard that he just barely got the words out, and at this point I couldn't stop laughing. "You know, you're one crazy bastard Gerald" I said this with absolute certainty, even after considering I just met him.

The Alice Cooper show was an amazing thing to experience live, right on the riverbed in the west bank of the flats, even with Gerald's crazy stories in between songs. In the year two thousand sixteen it felt unique to see a true pioneer of shock-rock perform, and I enjoyed every second, that was until it was time to disperse.

The night was coming to an end just like all good things eventually do, and the final chorus of School's Out echoed around the riverbed. The energetic crowd was now fleeing the scene and for some insane reason Gerald decided to sit for a moment and take a rest.

After he was nearly trampled a dozen or so times I convinced him to stand back up, so we could search for Jack and Sabrina. I spotted Jack about twenty feet five feet away, hanging on to the rail that led to the exit. I began to help guide Gerald towards the exit and when we neared Jack he informed us Sabrina was in the car, waiting.

Jack then grabbed a hold of Gerald's arm for balance, both appearing very drunk on top of the LSD, then they stumbled into the parking lot. "Aren't you coming?" Jack asked as he looked back at me.

"Sure, why not" I responded.

Chapter 3: Good Grief

The parking lot was shared between Nautica Pavilion and multiple restaurants/clubs in the flats, which led to a very odd mixture of Alice Cooper fans and hipsters. Jack and Gerald must have not even noticed the six inch curb that separates the lot from the sidewalk, as Jack fell to the ground.

Gerald nearly joined Jack, falling half way down before grabbing a hold of a small handicap parking sign that began bending to extreme measures, as his pants fell to his knees. A middle-aged social justice warrior type passe us, covering her teenage daughter's eyes while mumbling "Good grief".

"He has some serious screws loose" said another as they looked back several times in pure disgust. Sabrina luckily arrived in the car, pulling up swiftly and rescuing us as a security guard approached. We assisted Jack and

Gerald into the car, then we began to head west.

I soon realized where we were going, after Gerald demanded that Sabrina turn right, and it would be the last house, on the left... Gerald's house alone sounded like a bad idea, but what's this "last house on the left talk?" I wondered nervously.

We arrived at the house that looked near abandoned and had multiple junk trucks in the front yard. We walked up the near completely rotted stairs and into the terrible house. I instantly spotted a bucket in the center of the floor and he proclaimed "Don't go near my shit bucket!"

"No such plans Gerald" I replied.

"Gerald?" A woman's voice asked from the next room over, finally she came running in and hugging Gerald. "We missed you!" the woman assured him as two more women also joined us in the room. The women appeared worn-out, like they've seen their better days.

"You like my women?" Gerald asked.

'They're his street whores" Jack chimed in, "he's a real Hugh Hefner" he added while chuckling to himself before finishing "look it's not the best place to crash, but we're gonna have to make it work. He's got a phone, how about touch base with the magazine back in Nashville, see if they have anything else lined up".

I nodded cautiously and said "I believe I will sleep in the car".

There was no rejection so I went to the car and slept briefly, before being woken up by a knock on the window. I assumed it was one of Gerald's "whores" who was trying to make a quick buck. I glanced over and was shocked to see Sabrina. "Sabrina" I said under my breath and rolled the window down.

"Jack's a complete bore right now, so... here I am" she said with a cute smirk on her face before continuing "can I get in?"

I was speechless, of course I found her attractive, but Jack was like family to me. "No, I'm sorry. I just wanna get a little sleep" I replied.

She then kicked the car and walked away angrily, saying "Fine, your loss".

At this point falling back a sleep was very unlikely, so I turned the car on to listen to the radio. I recall listening to the station and having no success, it was new country garbage. II began to assume Jack and Sabrina liked this new pop country trash and I nearly changed the station and then One Piece At A Time by Johnny Cash began to play. Now this is a song I thought, this song tells more of a story than one hundred pop country songs combined.

After listening to the song a very fast paced advertisement stated that David Allan Coe would be playing at the Agora Ballroom on

Euclid Avenue in Cleveland, Ohio the following week. The advertisement was maybe ten seconds long and played like an animated advertisement for some sort of monster truck show.

This is great I thought, I can use this as a chance to gather some more solid material to take back to Nashville with me. I found the entire situation odd, considering Coe was my favorite country artist and Jack was singing along to his song when we first met, and now here we are full circle. I called Volunteer Variety the following morning and pitched them a story that I was covering the final stage of Outlaw Country music. They enjoyed the pitch and gave me the green light.

Chapter 4: Last of a dying breed

In order to cover the current state of 'Outlaw Country' it is important to understand the complete history of the outlaw movement and what these artists stood for. The origin of outlaw country is a greatly debated topic amongst fans and historians alike. Some people believe the term was first coined by Hazel Smith (a writer from Nashville) while others believe the term was coined in more of a collective fashion over a period of time in the early 1970's. Hazel Smith used the term to describe the music coming out of Tompall Glaser's recording studio which was known as 'Hillbilly Central'.

There is also a debate as to what is considered 'Outlaw Country', with some fans believing the term describes country artists that were trying to break away from the watered down 'Nashville Sound' of the 1950's and 60's by writing songs of their choice instead of being pressured by producers. However other fans seem to think the term describes the type of music that was being played by these artists with themes such as drinking, gambling, prison, etc. being commonly used.

The origin of 'Outlaw Country' is hard to pinpoint, but the end unfortunately seems to be in near sight. There are not many outlaw country artists in today's music and only a few original outlaws are still alive. Willie Nelson, Billy Joe Shaver, Kris Kristofferson, Hank Williams Jr and David Allan Coe are the last original outlaws standing. Hank Williams Jr once referred to himself as a dinosaur in his song of the same name, and he's not too far off, in many ways he is one of the very last of a dying breed.

"An outlaw can be described as somebody who lives outside the law,
beyond the law, and not necessarily against it."
- Hunter S. Thompson

The early 1970's was an important time in country music and the birth of the outlaw movement, a sub genre in which the artist had more creative freedom and were influenced more by their peers and less by the record companies. Amongst these early pioneers was David Allan Coe, a country singer that fans have dubbed 'The Original Outlaw' which was also the title of his 1995 album. Coe has undoubtedly earned that title, performing outlaw music for nearly five decades with his career beginning in 1970 with his debut album 'Penitentiary Blues'.

The release of his debut album proved Coe was the real deal, but it wasn't until his 1974 album ' The Mysterious Rhinestone Cowboy' that he found his country stride. Unlike his debut album that he wrote in prison which was mainly blues oriented, his 1974 album was pure country. During the 1970's Coe was covering topics that most artists wouldn't dare attempt.

Coe wrote songs that were completely different than everyone in the industry, and that was because he was different. Coe spent nearly twenty years incarcerated throughout the state of Ohio, upon his release he lived in a hearse that he parked in front of The Grand Ole Opry.

A great amount of Coe's success is of course due to Johnny Cash, who inspired nearly every artist in the outlaw genre. Cash influenced several prisoners with his frequent performances in various prisons around the country. Cash was a very early pioneer to the genre with his 1953 hit 'Folsom Prison Blues', although labeled as 'rock-a-billy' it shares many of the same elements as outlaw country.

Cash later In his career was part of the outlaw country supergroup 'The Highwaymen', consisting of fellow outlaw singers Willie Nelson, Kris Kristofferson and Waylon Jennings. Merle Haggard was also a frequent collaborator with Cash. The aforementioned Merle Haggard was directly inspired by Johnny Cash, when Cash performed at San Quentin Prison while Haggard was currently serving time.

Haggard has a great claim to kick-starting the outlaw movement with his 1968 song titled 'Mama Tried' which was a couple years prior to the term outlaw country being coined but the direction of the song was clear. Merle Haggard and his band 'The Strangers' were opening the door for the outlaw movement that was following in the coming years.

In order to understand the future of country music, we must study the past. It is important to cover the 1920-40's before covering the heart of the outlaw movement in the 1970's. The early 1970's may have been when the term was coined, but the roots of outlaw country tie all the way back to early country artists like Jimmie Rodgers, The Carter Family, Ernest Tubb and Hank Williams.

These artists were significant influences on the outlaw country sub-genre, they were true pioneers who were groundbreaking in their own way and helped carve the not so taken path. The Carter Family was the first family in country music and were amongst the original artists performing hillbilly music in the 1920's.

Jimmie Rodgers was known as 'The Father of Country' with his early 1927 song 'Blue Yodel No.1 (T for Texas, T for Tennessee) being widely considered the first country hit. The 1940's saw a new surge in country music with the 1941 Ernest Tubb classic 'Walking The Floor Over You'.

The legendary Hank Williams also had his big hit this decade with the 1947 'Move It On Over'. Hank Williams and his band of 'Drifting Cowboys' are perhaps the most important and influential piece of country music history.

By 1974 the term 'Outlaw Country' has now been coined, as evident by Waylon Jennings 1974 album 'Ladies Love Outlaws'. This was Jennings second album that would fall into the subgenre with the first being his 1972 album 'Good Hearted Woman'.

During this time Willie Nelson, a future frequent collaborator of Jennings, was releasing his 1973 album 'Shotgun Willie'. Nelson and Jennings are true originals of the outlaw movement and Nelson broke into the mainstream and became widely known as the most popular of the outlaws.

In a sub-genre that is so rare and unique, the similarities among the outlaw artists are shocking. Despite the obvious that the outlaws were typically against the system and most have been in trouble with the law, nearly every artist in the outlaw movement was born in the 1930's.

The connection between the original outlaws and the Depression Era seemed obvious, as growing up in this era likely formed them into the outlaws they became. Country music had many important milestones over the last century.

The 1920's had The Carter Family and Jimmie Rodgers, the 1940's had Ernest Tubb and Hank Williams and the 1930's gave birth to Johnny Cash, Willie Nelson, Kris Kristofferson, Johnny Paycheck, Waylon Jennings, Merle Haggard, Billy Joe Shaver and David Allan Coe.

Billy Joe Shaver and Kris Kristofferson never seemed to get quite enough credit for their crucial part of the outlaw movement. They were greatly respected by their peers in the sub-genre and had a cult-like following but not as widely known by the average fan.

Both artists were more songwriter than singer but they were among the best as evident by Shaver's instant classic 'Wacko From Waco' and Kristofferson and Rita Coolidge hit 'Dakota The Dancing Bear'.

Johnny Paycheck also played a significant role with the developing outlaw songs of the 1970's. Paycheck's first big hit was the 1972 song title 'She's All I Got' followed by his 1977 song 'Take This Job And Shove It' which was written by David Allan Coe.

George Jones was another artist who inspired the outlaw movement with his 1959 pro-moonshine hit ' White Lightning'. Jones was an incredibly successful country artist and had another huge hit twenty four years later with his 1983 'Tennessee Whiskey', which was a song David Allan Coe recorded two years prior and they performed together live at Farm Aid.

Jones was very active during the 1970's outlaw era and was very respected by his fans and peers alike for his musical talent and unique voice.

The 1970's was one of, (if not) the greatest era in the history of country music. A new sub-genre was introduced known as 'Outlaw Country' and some of the greatest country songs of all time were recorded. Country classics such as, 'You Never Even Called Me By My Name', Long Haired Redneck', 'I'm A Ramblin Man', 'Are You Sure Hank Done It This Way', 'Luckenbach Texas', 'Whiskey River', 'I'm The Only Hell Mama Ever Raised', 'Family Tradition', 'Man In Black', 'One Piece At A Time', 'Ramblin Fever' and so many more.

There were three states that played the largest role in contributing to outlaw country music (Ohio, Tennessee and Texas). David Allan Coe was born in Ohio, which he will remind you of in several songs, including his song titled 'Ohio Boy'. Johnny Paycheck was also born in Ohio close to the same time as Coe and both served time in Ohio prisons. Although several artists were born and formed in Ohio, the outlaw sound was created in Tennessee and Texas respectively.

Nashville, Tennessee was always the heart of country music and outlaw country was no different. Texas played a big role with several outlaw artists born in the lone star state including Willie Nelson, Waylon Jennings, Billy Joe Shaver and several others. Tennessee and Texas are very similar with both states populated with a great amount of country fans and both states have the two largest stages in country, The Grand Ole Opry and Live At Billy Bobs.

  The following week I went to the ticket office and bought four tickets at the cost of twenty five dollars per ticket. I gave the extra tickets to Jack, Gerald and Sabrina, and rode with them to the show because the Agora ballroom was only about eight blocks from Jack's.

In order to accurately cover the outlaw movement from a journalistic point of view I deemed it necessary to experience a live show and this was the only chance I would likely get.

When we arrived I was quite shocked by the opening act, it was some sort of Nu Metal that was obviously still in the development stage. As I looked around trying to see how the crowd was reacting to this below average band I noticed that most of them already seemed too drunk to realize what was going on.

The crowd was a strange mixture of bikers, metalheads and several older fans. The amount of people in the ballroom during the start of the show was maybe fifty people, including the three I brought with me. The band was very bad, almost to the point that I felt sorry for them. This was their chance I thought, to open for a real legend and they are completely blowing the opportunity. The band was some sort of local group from what I gathered.

The opening act played, kind of, to less than fifty people. I was very close to the stage with the group I was with, because we wanted to get front row before the crowd came. If we would have known the opening act would be this awful we would have delayed our arrival time.

Not only was the band terrible, but they were making very awkward eye contact with us, they seemed to be seeking some sort of approval. Perhaps they wanted us to engage in the show and head bang or begin moshing to the awful sounds they were creating. We decided to use this time wisely and headed towards the back door which led to the parking lot. We figured we would smoke a few joints and return.

Upon returning we were appalled to find the opening act still playing. They have been playing for what seemed like eternity, but was probably closer to one hour. Now the ballroom was becoming more populated, with the fan count nearing close to what looked like around five hundred people.

The crowd still had the same quality of fans. Bikers with their outlaw colors on, metalheads and a few older hillbillies who were clearly there for a country performance. As the crowd packed in the fans became more anxious and impatient. The drunks that didn't seem to notice earlier, have definitely begun to take notice now. After the opening act crept over the one hour mark nearly half of the crowd began booing, while many others started chanting "D-A-C, D-A-C, D-A-C!".

The opening act seemed to acknowledge the demands and finished their set very quickly after the chants began. Before leaving the stage the band declared "And now the man you all came to see, the legend David Allan Coe". The place erupted with cheers, people began high fiving while others chugged their beer.

Finally, after a few minutes of setting up the stage correctly David Allan Coe entered. Coe could barely walk and needed help to a chair that was placed on the center of stage. When he sat down he talked very briefly and began his set. As soon as he started singing I immediately forgot about the terrible band that opened the show.

I was blown away with his performance, Coe was in his mid seventies but played just like he did in the 70's. He played nearly all of his classics, while also covering classics of some other legends. As he was singing his songs the crowd was going crazy, they loved it. Even the ones that clearly didn't know much about him were loving it.

Throughout the night he played hits like 'Please Come to Boston', 'Tennessee Whiskey', 'Willie, Waylon and Me', 'Longhaired Redneck', 'You Never Even Called Me By My Name' as well as performing one of the greatest covers I've ever heard singing Waylon Jennings song 'Amanda'.

In between each song you could hear several drunks shouting "Play the dirty songs", referencing his 2 underground albums. As the night was obviously nearing the end, Coe began to talk to the excited crowd. He thanked them for coming out, then Coe began to educate them that he was born in Ohio.

He stated that he was "Born in Akron, and lived in Cleveland for a while, moved to Nashville and stayed in Texas" he paused and listened to the overwhelming approval of the crowd. Then he stated "What I'm trying to tell you is, I'm an Ohio boy", which led into his song titled 'Ohio Boy'. The fans erupted, What a way to end the show I thought.

After the show was over I thought about the history I just witnessed. This was truly one of the last original outlaws that was still alive, let alone still performing. The state of Outlaw country was basically summed up by this one single show. The genre is near extinction, when a legend like Coe only draws roughly five hundred people in the state he is from, shows the fan base is not what it once was.

The end of an era is inevitable. David Allan Coe had about as long of a ride as anyone else in the genre. A career spanning nearly five decades and now he will hopefully have some artist to pass the torch to. Coe did venture into projects with the new generation, performing songs with Kid Rock and Hank Williams 3. Coe also was part of the first metal/country crossover with the metal band Pantera.

Pantera was one of the biggest metal bands of the 90's, known as the outlaws of metal. Coe along with three members of Pantera formed the supergroup 'Rebel Meets Rebel', which was also the name of the album they released together. This album is a complete mixture of Outlaw Country and Heavy Groove Metal. Hank 3 also played drums for one song on the album.

David Allan Coe recorded a song called 'Outlaw Ways' with Hank 3, which in many ways seemed like the passing of the torch. Hank 3 is definitely one of the few new generation country singers that can be considered an outlaw. Just like his dad and grandfather did before him, he is blazing his own trail.

Hank 3 started a new sound, a sound that can only be described as 'Hellbilly' which was a term previously used by, and to describe Rob Zombie. Hank 3 also performs outlaw country that is reminiscent of the old stuff from the legends before him. The best example of this would be his song titled 'Country Heroes' where he pays his respect to the original outlaws.

Kid Rock is another artist who Coe passed the torch to. Although Rock, similar to Coe, didn't start in the country genre he has sure made an impact. It all started when he became friends with Coe. Rock said he always admired Coe's work and mentions him in his song 'American Badass'. Coe has also written several songs for Kid Rock including 'Single Father' and 'Only God Knows Why'.

Coe was not the only outlaw who became friends with Rock. Hank Williams Jr. also formed a bond with Rock and performed several songs together like 'Redneck Paradise' and a live version of 'Family Tradition'. Williams has also appeared in Rock's music video 'M-F Quite Like Me'. When an artist is real and authentic you can sense it.

That's the problem with a lot of new wave country, the artists haven't lived a life of an outlaw. The Outlaw Country scene sadly seems to be nearing the end of the road, but as Dimebag Darrel and Vinnie Paul once said "The songs will live on long after we are all gone".

**Demon Rats:
A Shocking Journey
into the
Liberal Pits of America**
A Short Story
By Carl E Miller

Introduction:

In order to cover the average Democratic Liberal, I deemed it necessary to study them in their natural habitat. After several months of close observation from various news outlets that covered fiery-but-mostly-peaceful-protest, I felt obligated to get out there and witness this circus first-hand for myself.

I figured if I'm going to make the most of this trip and piss some people off, then who better to bring along with me than my two hundred and fifty pound, extremely hyper hillbilly friend Brandon from West Virginia. At first I wondered where I would go for some of the best up-close action, so I looked through a map and highlighted some areas that I would normally want to avoid all together.

I called Brandon and told him my plans, he was ready, like always, so I assured him I would be at his place to pick him up in the morning and we would be headed to Cleveland, Ohio from there.

"Cleveland, huh? Hell that's a great choice, a real Liberal shit hole, and we can get there in what, six hours or so?" He asked.

"That's the plan." I responded quickly.

"Well alright, once we get to Cleveland I know a guy, his name is Worm and he can show us the real underground. We can get a great read on these fuckers." Brandon said as I agreed. I then hung up the phone and began to pack my bags, it felt like I was headed to a third world country but I have to see for myself what's lurking in the bowels of America.

Chapter 1: Shuckin' and Jivin'

September, 2020

I pulled up to Brandon's house around 7:00 a.m, sounded the horn twice and watched as he charged through his front door and jumped into my truck anxiously.
"Man, I'm ready!" He exclaimed as we began to head north, towards Cleveland. I turned on the radio to kill some time, and a classic song (Me and Crippled Soldiers) by Merle Haggard was playing.

A very fitting song for the times I thought, the song was more or less about people burning the American flag, and him and crippled soldiers being the only ones who seem to give a damn about it. The song was released in 1990, in direct response to the United States Supreme Court decision that allowed the burning of the American flag, citing First Amendment rights.

We listened to numerous songs of the same nature and arrived in Cleveland a little quicker than we originally planned, the time flew by listening to some good old Merle Haggard and Waylon Jennings tunes. After touching down in Cleveland we decided to first visit the dreaded east side. Brandon has been to Cleveland before and said he knew where all the gritty parts were for us to explore.

We first drove to a street called Lexington Ave. Where League Park is located, former home stadium of the Cleveland Indians. We circled the ballpark several times, then we received our first glimpse of the city life as we noticed a strange looking woman. She was sitting on the rotting front porch of an abandoned house, her legs were spread open, she had a short dress on and what appeared to be a very bad case of staph infection.

"Hey boys!" She yelled as we sped past waving, trying our best to not be rude.

"Hell, your birthday is coming up Brandon, I can get you an early present." I suggested.

"I wouldn't fuck her with your dick." He quickly replied.

We then drove to a street called St. Clair Ave. near downtown, we turned sharply into a little brick alley, where a dirty homeless-looking man was sitting on a stool. We pulled up slowly, barely having enough room to pass him as Brandon rolled his window down and stared at the man. "Can I have some money?" The man asked as we just watched him.

Finally Brandon replied very calmly, "No way." Then suddenly the man stood up and started making crazy gestures with his arms, like some sort of gang signs.

"Man, you always say that!" The dirty man exclaimed.

"I know." Brandon replied very earnestly.

"Have you seen him before?" I asked Brandon as he shook his head laughing. We soon had enough of this encounter and drove past him, I glanced in the rear-view mirror and watched as he was still back there shuckin' and jivin' in the alley.

We started to make our way to the midtown area of Cleveland, passing multiple women in front of a woman's shelter who seemed to have pissed themselves, their crotch areas soaked.

"Them girls are already wet and ready." I said as Brandon smiled, acknowledging my wisdom. We then found ourselves turning onto a street called Lakeside Ave.

Chapter 2: Scram, Ya Crumb Bum

"Stay alert around here, this is where the men's homeless shelter is." Brandon said in a very serious manner. Moments later we already witnessed our first crime, as several people dressed in all black jumped a barbed wire fence carrying suitcases. They used towels to cover the barbed wire, and once they hit the street they scattered like cockroaches after turning the lights on.

This was quite a scene and we observed it for a while, until the gun shots began. Then we took off like we were the ones robbing, as we burned the tires and tried our best to not get shot.

"You'll get that in the big city" Brandon said this while chuckling, as we regained our sense of humor once we were a few blocks away. We continued driving and found ourselves near some sort of male swinger bar, two men were out front embracing as I yelled at them "Gay!".

"Look up there." Brandon said as I noticed a crackhead running down the street with a hot water tank about fifty yards away.

"That's a strong son-of-a-bitch!" I exclaimed as Brandon agreed. We pulled up next to him and I started shouting, "Hey you, scumbag! Put your hands up and step away from the hot water tank." The crackhead didn't even flinch and continued running, likely on his way to get his fix.

"Man these fucking crackheads and whores outnumber the real people in this worthless city." Brandon said while pointing out another crackhead who was looking around nervously, before finally pulling a weed whacker out of his very large, baggy jacket. I don't even know how he got the damn thing in his clothes, but he did.

Another man drove past on a bicycle, he was carrying two other bikes that he likely just finished stealing. We watched for several minutes before Brandon suggested, "Let's go to Worm's house now, he should be home."

He entered the address into the GPS and we began to head to the west side. We were directed down a few side streets, then through the west bank of the Flats. While passing by a church I noticed several older women that were dispersing from mass, dressed for the occasion in their nice clothes. Then the comedy began as the women hit the street and we watched as a homeless man was squatting in the near-by bushes, taking a shit reading the Sunday newspaper.

The women rushed past the man, ignoring him like he had the plague, or in this year the coronavirus. Another bum was on the corner, digging into the city garbage can that was overflowing. "The good stuff is at the bottom!" I yelled as we drove past him.

"Hey, fuck you!" The bum shouted back as we continued down West 25th Street.

Brandon yelled back at him, "Scram, ya crumb bum!"

Nearly all of the businesses were unfortunately boarded up due to the Black Lives Matter riots and the section eight style houses were all condemned now.

"Man, this city can't take much more. It's already on the brink of death." I said as Brandon nodded.

Chapter 3: Worm's House

"Wait until you see where we're going next." Brandon said as the GPS signaled to turn right on Lorain Ave. "This is about as low down and gritty as it gets. Nothing but whores, crackheads, heroin addicts, pill junkies and bums. These types of people would love the Socialism/Communism agenda from the Biden/Harris ticket."

Within about five minutes we spotted a one-legged hooker that was leaning against a wall. This can't be real life I thought as I went to point her out to Brandon, but he already noticed the hooker and was in the process of rolling his window down before I could say anything.

"Hop in." Brandon suggested as the hooker grinned and began to literally hop towards us. "Go, go!" Brandon shouted at me as I began to accelerate, leaving the hooker back there cussing us out. "Man, I don't know which part of town is worse anymore." He added as the GPS said to turn in an alley and we would be arriving at our destination.

"Here it is, Worm's house. He's a regular hillbilly Hugh Hefner. All the street whores stay at Worm's, if you want the Cleveland underground then here it is." Brandon said as we began to walk to the front door. He knocked, barely touching the door, and it suddenly opened. "Hey, Worm. This is my buddy Paul and he wants to see the gritty side of Cleveland. He's doing a study on Liberal shit hole cities, and wants to cover all walks of the street life.*

"Well just don't fucking stand there! Come in." Worm offered as we obliged. "But don't be calling me fucking Worm, I go by my first name Gerald." He said as he showed us through his near abandoned, three story house. "This is where all the action takes place." He added as he pointed at a huge charred-up mattress on the floor that appeared to have been in a fire. The house was quite a site, but I was looking for more excitement.

We looked around a little longer, as he gave us a tour and pointed out important landmarks like his "shit bucket" and his makeshift bathtub. "Who do you want to win the upcoming election, Trump or Biden?" I asked Gerald as we began to leave his house.

"Neither, I'm ready for the revolution." He said with a demented grin. "Maybe I'll see you boys tonight at the bonfire." He added before closing his door. We drove away, examining buildings that were marked "BLM" and "No justice, no peace" on Lorain Ave.

Where does all the damn spray paint come from? Is there a new law that requires food stamps to cover paint products? Have the Liberals deemed it a necessity? I wondered this to myself as we drove around in Cleveland's west side in sheer disgust.

Nearly every street we drove down had boarded-up houses, broken glass in the streets, graffiti everywhere and a God awful smell. I'd like to think the city looked much better before the riots but I doubt it, considering the city hasn't had a Republican Mayor in over thirty years, and only three Republican Mayors total since 1941.

Chapter 4: Liberal Heaven

There seems to be a similar scenario in most cities that have been completely run into the ground. In this country we don't just necessarily have a problem, we have a Liberal problem, a Democrat problem if you will. The next destination on this trip through Hell would be a quick stop to the Steelyard Commons, to visit the worst Wal-Mart in the country.

The Steelyard Commons was a shopping plaza that was about a five minute drive away, and when we arrived in the massive parking lot we found the true Liberal hangout. There were cars double parked everywhere, mainly as close to the store as possible, with Biden/Harris bumper stickers proudly planted on the backs of them.

"This is it, Scum Central." I said in a bittersweet tone. The first few people we spotted were sporting trendy face masks that read "I can't breathe", which we both thought was very ironic to say the least.

"If you can't breathe, then take the damn mask off!" Brandon shouted at one as we drove past. We parked a good distance away from the rest of the vehicles and sat in our truck, simply observing the scene. A con-artist type approached us with a necklace in his hand.

"Are you guys interested in a 14 karat gold chain?" He asked as he began torching it with a cheap crack lighter to prove its validity.

"No, we're looking for the Democrat paradise. We heard it might be down here in the Steelyard Commons." I said as he seemed confused.

"I think you just short-circuited his brain." Brandon whispered as I tried to think of something to say.

"Look, we don't want your chain but we'll give you ten bucks to run head first into that blue car over there with the Biden/Harris bumper sticker." I said as he began to drool, nodding his head eagerly and holding his hand out.

"The money first!" He demanded.

"No. You do the job, you get the..." I said but before I could even finish the sentence, he took off full speed. He ran like a prime Usain Bolt, head first into the car as the alarm started to echo through the crowded parking lot. He hit the ground very hard and didn't move again, then Brandon started yelling at me, "Come on start the truck, let's go to the other side of the parking lot."

We drove in a hurry to the other side, parked and began to make our way to the entrance. Two security guards were blocking the door and we noticed a line was formed. "We've reached full capacity, you have to put a mask on and get to the back of the line." One of the guards said as I brushed off his comments with a slight wave of my hand, signifying my disapproval.

"We didn't come to buy anything anyway, we just came down here to simply observe." I replied.

"Observe what?" The guard asked.

"An observation of Liberals in their natural habitat." I responded quickly.

"What the fuck!" Said a nearby woman.

"Look, we're doing a report on Biden supporters. We're writing a story about them, no Democrats were harmed in the making of this story. It's an innocent take on their everyday life." I assured her as she glared back at me.

"You better get the fuck outta here, before you get hurt cracker!" She shouted at me.

"What's the problem here?" Brandon said before continuing, "Are you prepared to fight one of Worm's girls?" He asked as the lady said nothing for a moment, then she finally replied.

"Is that how you treat a woman who's been in the Army?" She responded as Brandon laughed.

"Lady, the only Army you've been in, is the Salvation Army." Brandon replied as the crowd was growing angry, they began chanting and throwing things in our direction. The scene started to appear violent, especially if we stuck around much longer, so we had to make a decision.

"Well, now is as good of a time as any to make our way back to Republican ground."
I suggest as Brandon agreed.

"We've seen all this city has to offer." Brandon said as we began to head to the truck so we could leave. We saw up-close and personal how the average big city Liberal lives. Now with the information we've gathered, we will head back to a red city with a better understanding of the Demon Rats.

Chapter 5: Liberal Cities Look Better in the Mirror

Reflecting back on what we saw, there is no doubt it's time for Cleveland to get a Republican in office and clean these streets. If there is anything to gain from visiting a Democrat city, it's the knowledge that comes with it for future comparisons to Republican cities.

In the year 2020 nothing is surprising, except perhaps the election results of course. Now for anyone who has been watching the news for the past eight months, it should come to no surprise that we live in a very divided country. That being said, Joe Biden supporters in general confuse me greatly, so I was thankful that I have come to understand the enemy slightly better.

Now the common Democrat is not that hard to figure out, most of them start off simple. They typically use free health care, equal rights, global warming and currently the pandemic as talking points, but fixing them issues will not satisfy the self-proclaimed victim that is the average democrat.

These modern Democrats have gone too far, for most acknowledging they were wrong is unfathomable. For others, acknowledging they were wrong would mean being outcast from their inner city circles. However where the liberals got it right was their strategy, by creating groups such as Black Lives Matter it becomes nearly impossible to have outspoken public opposition. To oppose Black Lives Matter to the uneducated, would seem like a racist viewpoint.

Another clever trick that they have mustered up was with Antifa. They call themselves anti-facsist, yet they use the exact same techniques as fascist. By destroying monuments, burning flags, ridding of history books, changing city and street names, looting stores, declaring everyone who doesn't agree with them as maggots, these are all techniques used by fascist.

In one breath, the clever Democrat will be pro-abortion and justify it with the age-old saying "Her body, her choice." Then in the same breath they will tell you to "Put a mask on!" That you're putting others at risk, ironic don't you think? These are the same people who call Trump rallies superspreader events, but watch Black Lives Matter and Antifa burn, loot and kill in nearly every major city for seven plus months and never mention the pandemic.

When they use the name Black Lives Matter it gives them more room to get away with crime, for example as of November, 2020 it is estimated that the group is responsible for more than two billion dollars in damage across America. Dozens of officers have been killed by the group and worst of all is the Biden/Harris administration were bonding these terrorists out of jail, so they could do it again.

Now that all of their cases have fallen apart to prove that the "Evil white man was out to get them." Black Lives Matter still clings on to a loyal, but very dumb fan base. Are there racist cops? Sure. There are racist in every profession, in all walks of life. Can't escape that, but to pretend that cops are targeting minorities at an incredible amount more than white people is ignorant.

All statistics across the board show fairness. Do more black people die by police than white? No!

Do more black people get killed at a higher percentage than whites, by cops? Yes, and that is because they're committing more crime and not following orders given to them by the police officer. You see it isn't a great idea for rap groups like the NWA and others to make songs about "Fuck the police!" Then they cry when they commit crimes and police arrest them.

So in order to move forward in a positive way, we needed Trump. Not only as a country but the world needed him, he's not gone of course and he certainly can still deny seceding, or win major court battles. We will see, I will keep my spirits and hope alive and no no matter what we will rise back stronger. That being said we have our work cut out for us. Biden/Harris will now lay claim as the victors of a fraudulent election, and with that will come their Socialst/Marxist/Communist beliefs.

Our country was founded on Capitalism, and we have seen what has happened to countries that have tried it the Biden/Harris way, they failed. We saw what eight years of Obama/Biden did to America, which is what led to the rise of Trump to begin with. Now we are taking multiple steps back, both literally and figuratively. Biden is nearing eighty years old, spending more than half of that time as a politician and accomplishing nothing noteworthy.

In America, we have short tension spans and we forget where our problems originated. Black Lives Matter started in 2012 under Obama/Biden, after the Trayvon Martin killing. The cages that were built that stored the illegal immigrants children in were built under Obama/Biden. It seems most things that the right is blamed for the left in fact did. Hillary Clinton called Trump a Russian spy for years, then it turns out she colluded with Russians.

The irony and hypocrisy are on full display this year, to the point where people are now flocking to hear what Alex Jones has to say because come to find out he's been right the entire time. Not a big surprise, considering he's been censored and banned from every major social media platform because the tolerable left who allign with anti-facsist use Nazi techniques to silence their political opponents.

Maybe the biggest lie of them all is how the media lies to the viewer and puts fear into their hearts simply to boost ratings. They inflate covid cases and tell you that Trump rallies are racist and minorities aren't welcome. Then we find out everyone is welcome, even protestors walk freely among them without being attacked. A Trump rally is one massive party with Americans having fun, and the left are too busy belly-aching about free healthcare to join the fun.

So everyone is welcome at a Trump rally but Kaitlyn Bennett can't go to a college campus and interview people without thousands of rabid Black Lives Matter cowards trying to attack her. It's pathetic and un-American and shouldn't be tolerated any longer. It's a shame that it's gone on this long. In Washington, D.C there were several hundred thousand Trump supporters who descended into the streets to protest the fraudulent election.

After the actual peaceful protest by real Americans, they dispersed and when the crowd grew small Black Lives Matter appeared and attacked several women and young girls. After hearing about the attack and not being too far away, the Proud Boys, a right-wing patriot group turned around to confront the Black Lives Matter terrorist. Let's just say it didn't go very well for the terrorist scum, we will just leave it at that.

So when I grew up I was always told the oldest saying is "An eye for an eye," and with that wisdom I say God bless Trump and the Proud Boys, it's about time. Now looking forward I of course want nothing but the best for my country, but I am no fool. If Biden/Harris get into office we will have a serious uphill battle in front of us.

Trump was for the average man, no matter how many times the fake news likes to tell you otherwise. It's no secret that nearly every news outlet, Hollywood actor, celebrity athlete, pop-star, elitist all want Biden/Harris to win, not to mention Bill Gates and George Soros. The time has come to take America back and let them know that we won't stand for their Communist sell-out plan.

The ties with pedophilia to the current Democratic party are undeniable, with more examples coming out every day. The most recent example of this being Hunter Biden's laptop from Hell, where he is rumored to be photographed nude with presumably underage women. We have to say no to Marxism, Socialism, Communism and this anti-white social justice warrior agenda they're trying to lay on us.

We need to beat them, politically of course. We need to open eyes around the world and expose the truth and hope it sets us free. We need our

pride back, our dignity, our patriotism, our strength, our leadership, our country.
Trump2020 and forever. At this point it's become a lifestyle, our great country is under attack….
The end

Made in the USA
Columbia, SC
01 May 2021